MW00587361

Philosophical Thinking is Yoga for the Mind®

Upper West Side Philosophers, Inc. provides a
publication venue for original philosophical
thinking steeped in lived life, in line with our
motto: *philosophical living & lived philosophy.*

HARNESSING
the POWER *of*
UNHAPPINESS

Wilhelm Schmid

Translated from the German by Karen Leeder

Upper West Side Philosophers, Inc.

New York · 2014

Published by Upper West Side Philosophers, Inc.
P. O. Box 250645, New York, NY 10025, USA
www.westside-philosophers.com / www.yogaforthemind.us

English translation copyright © 2014 by Upper West Side
Philosophers, Inc.
Originally published as *Unglücklich sein: Eine Ermutigung*
Copyright © Insel Verlag Berlin 2012
Author photograph copyright © 2013 by Jonathan Schmid

All rights reserved. No part of this publication may be repro-
duced, stored in a retrieval system, or transmitted, in any form
or by any means, electronic, mechanical, photocopying, record-
ing, or otherwise, without prior permission in writing from
the publisher. For all inquiries concerning permission to reuse
material from any of our titles, please contact the publisher in
writing, or contact the Copyright Clearance Center, Inc.
(CCC), 222 Rosewood Drive, Danvers, MA 01923, USA
(www.copyright.com).

The colophon is a registered trademark of Upper West Side
Philosophers, Inc.

Library of Congress Cataloging-in-Publication Data

Schmid, Wilhelm, 1953-
[Unglücklich sein. English]
High on low : harnessing the power of unhappiness / trans-
lated from the German by Karen Leeder.
pages cm. -- (Subway line ; No. 8)
Originally published as Unglücklich sein.
ISBN 978-1-935830-28-3 (alk. paper)
1. Happiness. 2. Well-being. 3. Melancholy. I. Leeder,
Karen J. II. Title.
BF575.H27S3613 2014
152.4'2--dc23

2013032345

Typesetting and Design: Michael Eskin

Contents

Foreword

"Today is just not my day!" If you can say that you're in luck. For many people it lasts much longer than a single day. They have to live day in day out with misfortune, through no fault of their own. This is made worse by the fact that we live in an age where we are made to feel we should be happy all the time. It is broadcast from the billboards: "Happiness!" Ads proclaim: "How to be happy!" Brochures promise us: "Even more happiness!" You can even book it at the travel agent: "Happiness guaranteed!" The newspapers run with titles like "Get switched on to happiness" one week, only to ask the next, "Why aren't we getting happier?"

To avoid any potential misunderstanding: It is of course a symptom of progress that we can concern ourselves with happiness rather than survival or fulfilling our duties. But what happens when happiness itself becomes a duty? The hype about happiness has itself acquired a *nor-*

mative meaning; it reinforces a new norm for the individual: You must be happy or else your life isn't worth living. If you happen to be unhappy, you begin to wonder whether you are missing something, to question whether you are cut out for happiness at all. Clearly, you have failed. Everyone else seems to succeed at it; or at least to work hard at giving that impression. Envy consumes the unhappy. If the worldwide happiness industry is to be believed, they will never join the ranks of the happy who inhabit the planet.

The *tyranny of happiness* threatens to squeeze out any room for unhappiness. Anyone who dares to challenge the absolute power of happiness in our day-to-day lives will be faced with an uphill struggle. There is no doubt that obsessive pessimism is a pain. But ostentatious optimism is no laughing matter either. The unhappy are browbeaten to the point where they no longer dare to talk about how they are feeling, or even think about it, as that would be to indulge in negative thinking, whereas they feel they are duty-bound to see everything in a positive light.

What are the causes of these hysterical outbreaks of happiness? One is certainly the *flight into happiness*. As we feel external pressures impinging on us more and more, we seek all the more urgently to find happiness within: Am I happy? Why everyone else and not me? How can I become happy in the future? But pressing questions are also thrown up by the 'dark side' of happiness: How many are driven to unhappiness simply because they believe they should be happy? What about the many unhappy ones who have to contend not only with their own unhappiness but also with the exorbitant happiness of everyone else? Surely, they can only feel increasingly excluded, surrounded as they are by the apparently happy insisting ever more stridently on their own happiness?

The escalating paeans to happiness elicit these questions because they are, in part at least, and not to put too fine a point on it, *antisocial*. They are indifferent to what happens to those who fall through the 'happiness cracks', that is, those in our society – and even more so in the world at large – who are forced to endure the misery of adverse conditions. What about the drawbacks of happiness? Not an issue, the argument goes. And if so, people only have themselves to blame. They refuse to be happy. They don't try hard enough. They haven't read all the self-help books carefully enough. Perhaps they simply aren't capable of being happy due to some genetic flaw or social disadvantage. That's unfortunate, but "it's not my problem." The unhappy today are like modern-day lepers, treated as outcasts, everyone keeps a distance.

Haven't I myself contributed to the increased attention given to happiness with my own previous book *Happiness: Everything You Need to Know About It**? Maybe so, yet with the important rider that happiness is *not the most important thing in life*. My aim here is not, however, to deny that happiness is important, but to try and put it into

---

* *Glück: Alles, was Sie darüber wissen müssen, und warum es nicht das Wichtigste im Leben ist* (2007).

perspective. Happiness is important, but *meaning* is more important. That happiness is the be all and end all is a fairy tale told by those who want to use happiness to fill the void in modern life left by the absence of meaning. But it is simply not up to the job. In life, a bit of happiness is the icing on the cake, and anyone will be grateful if some comes his way. But it is best taken in moderation. The power of happiness has limits, and asking too much of it makes no sense at all.

Isn't the task of the *art of living* to contribute to *successful living* and to make people happy? Of course, but failure and unhappiness have a place in human life too; and not least because they cannot simply be banished from it. Success is not the only option; failure is always a possibility. I have noticed that I am always taken aback when people talk about successful living. One cannot simply claim success as a prize, it's not possible. The best we can hope for is partial success. And a beautiful, fulfilled life is not necessarily the same as a successful one. So why invest so much in happiness and success? What if happiness doesn't find me? What is left behind when happiness departs, when a project, a relationship, a career or an entire life runs aground?

This ubiquitous discussion of happiness feeds the illusion that there could be such a thing as a successful life or a successful relationship without losses or drawbacks along the way. That in turn leads people to feel doubly unhappy when things do in fact go wrong. If you set your heart on happiness at any price and balk at the merest suggestion of unhappiness, you will be even more distraught to learn there is no such thing as unblemished joy. Wrestling with all the setbacks will cost you the strength you might otherwise have used to get over them, and the resulting exhaustion increases the unhappiness even further.

The great historical almanac of humanity boasts a slim chapter on the subject of happiness and a very considerable volume devoted to the rest. The desire to improve this ratio is certainly something to be supported. Wanting to turn it around, however, is unrealistic. Being unhappy is not something peculiar to human beings; animals can most likely do it too. But people can dream of alternatives. They are capable of knowing that there are reasons for unhappiness, and if they cannot find any, that is all the more reason to be unhappy. There is no way back to an animal existence; the only hope for such people is to recognize the unique nature of being human. Only then can their lives become richer and, at the same time, easier.

The real challenge in life is not how to be happy. With just a little know-how and a bit of practice anyone can do it; even if it's only for a short time. It is much more difficult to come to terms with being unhappy, to accept it and to bear it. That is truly heroic! This is what constitutes the other and more significant part of the *art of living*; one which is much more interesting for many more people. At any given moment, there is more than a small minority of unhappy people. This book is dedicated to them – to honoring and encouraging them.

1
If Happiness Doesn't Find Me

More than anything happiness is a matter of *luck*.
Everyone needs a good deal of it to be happy.
Looking back over the course of one's life, it is
easy to see the many key points where unlikely
coincidences were at work. Not only was being
conceived already a matter of luck, but to the
very end chance continues to rule our lives,
which are dependent on random events: Some
turn out well — chance encounters, for example, that help us along the way. But we have to
live with the fact that chance cannot be summoned on cue. Things happen the way they happen. If they happen.

Chance is what befalls us, however it comes
about, and for good or for ill. In earlier times,
people were cautious enough to reckon with
both possible outcomes, for chance cannot possibly work only to one's benefit. You can reduce
the probability of misfortune through careful

planning, but you cannot eliminate it altogether. For instance, the German word *Glück*, which now means *luck* or *happiness*, derives from the Middle High German *Gelücke*, which originally designated the outcome of chance in both a positive or a negative sense. In ancient cultures the random nature of fortune in both these senses was at once honored and feared in the form of a goddess: *Tyche* in Greek, *Fortuna* in Latin. People could trace both good fortune and misfortune back to the same source and were thus able to accept both with equanimity.

Modern man only recognizes a positive turn of fate as luck. If we feel fate *isn't going* our way, it is grounds for disappointment and irritation – for unhappiness, particularly if we are repeatedly unlucky in gambling: "I never win anything." In the shadow of the lucky few who do win are the multitudes whom the prize eludes through no fault of their own. The only way to escape this disappointment and the unhappiness that follows is not to play at all. Naturally the price for this security is a reduction of excitement in life – perhaps in its own way also a kind of unhappiness.

But even when happiness falls into our lap, we are not necessarily to be envied. If we cannot *hold onto* that random good fortune, we will become unhappy in just the same way. If you believe that with a stroke of luck the main work is behind you, and sit back doing nothing to keep it, you will see happiness slip through your fingers. Snow is the perfect metaphor for this kind of happiness: If you believe you can hold onto it, you will simply see it melt away – think of love, for example, that ubiquitous game of chance. And if two people are lucky enough to have found happiness together, that certainly doesn't mean they will remain happy, nor that they can force happiness to stay by dint of willpower.

Sometimes even a happy accident can turn into its *precise opposite*; even something that seems like a stroke of good fortune can turn out to be bad, while misfortune can disguise good fortune. Thus, the protagonist of Max Frisch's novel *Homo Faber* is seized by a curious reluctance to board his connecting flight and is upset when he is asked to get on the plane at the very last minute. Unfortunately, the plane crashes; fortunately, all the passengers are saved ... which gives rise to a new story that will lead to tragic consequences ...

An overwhelming cause of unhappiness is when fate intervenes in ways that are negative from the outset: as *habitual ill luck*. In order to avoid any possibility of that, we would have to inure ourselves to every kind of chance. A comment by the seventeenth-century French philosopher Blaise Pascal says it all: "All the misfortunes of men derive from the simple fact that they don't know how to stay quietly in their room." This is the only way to ensure lifelong security. But what kind of life would that be? It is much more attractive to open oneself to chance, to expose oneself, at least cautiously, to the vagaries of life. And sometimes it's the unhappy accidents that open up new perspectives.

They offer a unique opportunity to try something out that may one day be useful.

People often attempt to attract good fortune in a quasi-magical way with various kinds of lucky charms, even when it patently doesn't always work. Some even seem to have a kind of *magnetism* when it comes to chance — they are jammy bastards or, at the other end of the spectrum, walking disasters, without there being any rhyme or reason to it. The statistical distribution of chance includes these extremes, and in every life there are times when we seem jinxed in small matters or large. It's not simply that one or two strokes of luck seem to acquire their own momentum and draw others in their wake to create "a winning streak." Misfortunes can also seem to pile up — "it's just my luck." If one success leads to another, we begin to believe we will always be on the bright side of life; a few failures and we feel consigned to gloom forever. Luck of both kinds will run out one day. All streaks can only last for so long.

Is there any sense to be discerned in the misfortunes, strokes of bad luck and accidents that befall us? Why does someone fall victim to a serious illness? Why him? Why now? Is it a punishment? If so, for what? Does an invisible hand control our destinies? Is it a matter of fate, brought down on us by someone or something? Just as many people in pre-modern cultures believed in fate, many in modern cultures believe there is no such thing. We cannot prove it either way. As human beings we have no way of surveying our lives from beginning to end, never mind world events, nor indeed the stars. These could also have some influence over what appears to be chance – in any case, that's what some people believe, even today.

Only one thing is certain; and that is that an event can be *interpreted* as fate, even when it is a purely random act of chance. Choosing to see a pattern in it, as soon as it can no longer be undone, allows us to focus all our powers on making the best of a bad lot. It is up to each of us to stop struggling in vain and to say instead: "That is now my fate. It is what it is; and who knows what will come of it." Not every potential twist of fate has to be accepted of course. It is in our power to change many things, as for example the probability of becoming ill or how an illness might progress. But not everything can be controlled. Not every illness can be held at bay forever.

It is no great achievement to accept a stroke of good fortune that appears out of the blue and lands in our lap like a gift from the gods. It is much harder on the other side of the street, where there is nothing but bad breaks and any kind of acceptance costs us dear. Being unhappy and bearing misfortune stoically is something that many do not only for themselves but for others as well, as for example when there is something to be learned from being treated for a specific illness that will benefit others or protect them from similar misfortune. Countless improvements have come into being in this way; for no technology can function perfectly straight off. People learn by experience, and that experience will consist in good measure of things going wrong. Moreover, it's about trying to make a certain kind of chance misfortune less likely through individual or social prevention; but it will never be possible to banish it completely from human existence.

2
Does Happiness Always Make Us Happy?

Loving life, getting enjoyment from it — these are wonderful things. But they are not possible for all people all the time. People can go quite some way towards securing their own happiness; but for every moment of feeling good there is the potential to feel bad, for every pleasant experience there is an unpleasant one, for every happiness there is a matching unhappiness. And the more we fixate on our own well-being, the greater the potential for disaster. If our happiness is bound up in good health, then even a cold can make us unhappy. If having fun is the be all and end all, then an hour of boredom will bring everything crashing down. If we want to stay young at all costs, growing older will be more painful. Is life all about enjoyment? Then the prospect of the pain of visiting the dentist will blight the best part of a week in anticipation. Is success the only thing that counts? Then it just takes one failure to make life seem not worth living. Is the *art of living* about seeing the wonderful in everything? Then the mundane day-to-day that makes up the majority of our everyday lives becomes worthless. The *art of living* consists in living with that too.

Many hope to feel happy in love. Happiness!? In Love!? Is there any area of human life that more regularly makes people miserable almost regardless of what they consider love to be? If love is understood as the fulfillment of social obligations, it makes people unhappy because feelings don't come into play. If fulfillment is sought in beautiful sentiments, it causes unhappiness as soon as those feelings disappear temporarily or permanently. Does that mean it is better not to love at all? No, quite the contrary – there is almost nothing as meaningful as love. But human beings need a certain quantum of unhappiness, and love can be relied on to deliver.

Happiness in life and love is for many "the utmost pleasure." That's how John Locke defined it in *An Essay Concerning Human Understanding* of 1690. That set the bar so high that no one has been able to get over it since. It is the ambition to keep trying that drives the modern psyche. The "pursuit of happiness" that Locke ascribed to human beings found its way into the Declaration of Independence of 1776, and has since acquired the status of a basic right in a way that can only be dreamed of elsewhere. Some understand it to mean that the individual should have the right to achieve happiness on his own account and live as he sees fit, undisturbed by others, unimpeded by society or state. Others again insist on the importance of securing a basic provision for the individual in order to ensure that he does not spend his time in a constant struggle for survival and in order to make the pursuit of happiness possible at all.

For many the notion of the right to the *pursuit* of happiness becomes transformed into a *right to happiness* that should be underwritten by society and state in general – and life and love in particular. But how could such a legal enti-

tlement be made good? Should the state inter-
vene if I don't have the wherewithal to buy the
morning espresso that gives me a moment's
happiness — not to mention all the other things?
How do I claim the happiness due to me from
my loved ones? What sanctions can be brought
to bear? Modern man tends to make demands
of happiness that are both exorbitant and pre-
sumptuous. Immanuel Kant, in his *Observations
on the Feeling of the Beautiful and Sublime* of 1764,
had already insisted that we must "not make very
high claims on the joys of life or the perfection
of others."

Even Friedrich Nietzsche, who had mocked
the "little" happiness of the "last man" in *Thus
Spoke Zarathustra* of 1885 ("They have their little
pleasures for the day, and their little pleasures
for the night"), a few years later, in *On the Ge-
nealogy of Morals* of 1887, would go as far as
granting his imagined new men a *right to happiness*. They were to claim it as theirs simply, and
to assert themselves without any undue regard
for the unhappy people around them. Happiness

as a question of power — an intimation of times to come?

It might well be the case that humankind goes in search of happiness. But this pursuit is surrounded by darkness left, right and center. We pursue happiness because we are unhappy. Even if we find it, we cannot do without unhappiness — we need the contrast to our joy. For that reason any Gala TV show worth its salt that wants to keep its viewers sweet will not be able to do without at least some representations of misery. And the minute any period of happiness is over, we fall straight back into melancholy. Moments of happiness have a purpose in that they allow us to recover from bouts of unhappiness, but it makes no sense at all to wish for happiness all the time, as it simply cannot last forever. All the more unfortunate, then, that many look for exactly that from happiness: permanent wellbeing, constant joy, good spirits and lots of fun. But seeking in happiness a kind of perpetual state of pleasure is the surest way to become miserable.

No one can always be cheerful. The happiness hormones and endorphins that occur naturally in our bodies can do as little to change that as the stimulants and drugs we use to make ourselves feel better. In any case, the effect of these 'pick-me-ups' is often exaggerated. The effect of chocolate on the protective enamel of our teeth or our fat deposits is far greater than on our hormone balance, alas. Eating our favorite meal too often brings about tedium rather than pleasure. Even wellness can be overdone — our circulation doesn't wait for warning signals to be heeded. There is no doubt that sex makes you happy, but it is more often lacking in our lives than not — a situation that makes the person who is hoping for it unhappy at the very least. Someone who chases after every new fad to get the latest kick will realize too late that he has lost himself somewhere along the way; he must return to the painful search for himself.

The chemistry of happiness leads to unhappiness if it is overtaxed, for it involves substances that are quickly used up and have to be regenerated to take effect, only to become depleted again and so on … Thus, tired of happiness from time to time, the victims of our own *pleasure craze*, we become depleted and are happy to finally be able to wallow in a trough of despond that, unlike constant cheerfulness, demands nothing of us. Being miserable becomes our fallback position. At last we can enjoy the other side of things. The person who is down in the dumps might risk social death, nobody wants him around. But the one who is permanently in a good mood doesn't necessarily fare any better, wearing himself out hopelessly trying to perpetuate a sense of wellbeing while not noticing how he, too, becomes an imposition on those around him.

No one wants to call a halt when things are going well, but everyone has to come to terms with the fact that the good times can't last forever. They have to end so that they can return in a similar or different form in the future. The absence of the good times makes for a bad time in itself. Trying to put a gloss on the dark times no matter what serves only to make them last longer. Making room for feelings of disinclination, indisposition or malaise, on the other hand, turns such periods into times of regeneration in standby, as it were. Happiness can recover, regroup. The key thing is to properly acknowledge all the in-between times, the lulls and periods of hiatus. It is solely within the power of the individual to resist the *Zeitgeist*, the collective *happiness-jaunt* we are all on. Times change with the people who change.

It is common knowledge that at the very moment when the longed-for sense of wellbeing arrives at last, it can be immediately followed by a bout of depression. Pleasant and propitious circumstances promote happiness for as long as they are actively being sought and for a short while beyond that. But then the energy that has driven ambitions up to this point fizzles out. The person concerned doesn't know what has hit him: He has achieved everything he wanted – job, family, car, house. But that's the point exactly. What's next? With increasing prosperity comes the dawning anxiety that we might lose it all. The sense and certainty of our intimate relationships begins to erode. Why continue sticking together? Freed from old values, we are faced with new questions. What is right and what is wrong? As we enjoy ever greater freedom of choice, we are faced with the ever greater burden of having to make the choices and take responsibility for them in the first place. The many opportunities afforded to us in our day-to-day lives make us unhappy because life is too short to take advantage of them all, even though it's longer than ever before. So it is that the modern idea of happiness systematically drives us into unhappiness – therein lies its tragedy.

We doubtless have a vital interest in seeking out pleasure and avoiding pain. But it lies in the nature of things that we are not always successful. Pain, with few exceptions, tends to make us unhappy. We try to banish it from our lives, but it always arrives in some form or another: physical pain as a result of injury or illness, emotional pain as a result of disappointment or injured feelings, spiritual pain as a result of the meaninglessness we encounter when facing transience and death. There are means to relieve such pain, of course, but arsenals of analgesics do nothing to change the fact that such pain continues to exist.

It is possible, nevertheless, to change the *way we interpret* such pain. Doesn't it provide the contrast that allows us to feel pleasure more keenly? How would I know what pleasure feels like if I did not know pain? Aren't the most intense moments of happiness those we experience after pain subsides? Is it not pain that defines the clear contours of a reality that might otherwise become blurred? Does it not demand that we look at our lives afresh? What have I done – what have I perhaps done wrong? What really matters to me? On whom of those around me can I really rely? What remains of this life when it draws to a close? What will I leave behind? Of course it is possible to keep on reorienting oneself and redefining one's goals without pain, but hardly anyone does. We need a sense of emergency. Something has to hurt for us to feel troubled enough about the state of our lives to do something. And that's what we have unhappiness to thank for.

3
Farewell to Perpetual Contentment

Should your own country not be making any
preparations to enshrine happiness as a right,
then there is at least one bastion of hope: the
Kingdom of Bhutan. There, everything is geared
towards *gross national happiness*, something that
is certainly boosted by happiness tourism. Without closer inspection, however, we risk falling
into the *Bhutan trap*, that is, we risk disregarding
the most important precondition for happiness
in a Buddhist culture: an unquestioning acceptance of fate. This is an admirable concept of happiness, but one that is completely different from
modern culture, where fate has no place. After
all, the Bhutanese people experiences the down-
sides of happiness too: The injunction to wear
national costume, for instance, doesn't merely
serve the preservation of venerable traditions
but the mandated integration of Nepalese im-
migrants as well.

In many countries people measure their happiness simply in continued *survival*. In wealthy countries, people dream of the *good life*. This will bring them, they hope, a secure and enhanced form of contentment; while the products and services that allow them to achieve it increase the gross domestic product. Many people hope that luxury goods will keep the vagaries of life at bay. Luxury is the attempt to secure happiness at a higher material level and to dig oneself in behind the thick walls and towering battlements of a middle class *fortress* — the pursuit of bourgeois solidity in a literal sense. Yet in the simplest shack where people are exposed to life in the raw, there will probably, for all the inevitable misery, be greater reserves of happiness.

Against this background, the comparisons of relative happiness that appear everywhere these days are revealed in all their ludicrous splendor. People go chasing *maps of happiness* sponsored by *Institutes for Happiness* that sooner or later lead to *happiness overkill*. Any attempt to compare levels of happiness, however, cannot possibly be scientifically respectable – it's like comparing apples with oranges. There is no definition of happiness that would mean the same to everyone everywhere around the globe. Happiness as a concept is hermeneutically loaded and dependent on *interpretation* to an extreme degree. *Normative* presuppositions are open to question: Can one really speak of happiness in life? Is happiness really the same as contentment? Any science that relies on quantifiable evidence would also demand that studies should be *repeatable* and achieve the same verified results on different occasions. But from one day to the next countries are shifting about on the scale of happiness without having had a chance in such brief intervals to do much, if anything, to enhance or diminish their overall levels.

In Germany, for instance, one can consult an *Atlas of Happiness* to see the lay of the land. If the residents of Munich find themselves less happy than those of Hamburg, they can set about rectifying the situation. With enough effort at parties, in bars and in bed the scales can be tipped, while the day-to-day is all about keeping a low profile. The whole idea could be extended. Let them go head to head week on week! Who competes in the premier league and who in the second division of happiness? Who will win the annual happiness trophy? Who gets to play in the Champions League? Which nations will qualify to hold the World Championships of Happiness? At last we are distracted from the economic situation; our only concern the Triple-A of the ratings agencies of happiness. With a *hedonimeter* like the one designed by Francis Edgeworth in the nineteenth century, the degree of contentment of each and every individual can be measured minute by minute. But why only compare different groups of people? Why not humans and animals? Who is happier: man or sheep? And if it is the sheep, why not desire to be a sheep?

Everyone is entitled to achieving the level of *contentment* he desires. There is almost nothing nicer than being able to kick off one's shoes and sit back, satisfied with oneself, even if there is no particular reason for it, and satisfied with the world, even if everywhere one looks it shows no obvious sign of getting any better. But day in, day out? No doubt it would be good to live a charmed life in a perfect world, but in truth that could only be an incapacitated life in an immobilized world. It is no bad thing to be content now and again, but the art lies in not taking it too far. Lingering in a permanent state of laid-back euphoria becomes a problem. This has never been the driving force of change or improvement, quite the opposite: Satisfaction with one's lot and oneself brings progress to a halt.

For that reason it is problematic, to say the least, to draw people into a conspiracy of contentment and to make of it an ideology, a *contentology*, if you will. Happy people in a happy society run great risks. Their steady contentment stands in the way of the occasional necessity to be dissatisfied with reigning conditions; nobody could possibly want that. Should people who lack the most basic necessities of life be content, while others simply take what they please? What will become of the enviably contented existence of the inhabitants of the Vanuatu archipelago in the South Pacific if the sea levels continue rising? What would have become of Germany, had it simply sat back and done nothing when the PISA (Program for International Assessment) studies were published predicting total meltdown for Germany's education system. Fortunately, it reacted with extreme disquiet and, to the good fortune of all, sought to improve conditions. It is a good idea to complete a piece of work one has been given, and to complete it to the best of one's abilities, instead of constantly hankering for the happiness that contentment brings.

In any case, any attempt to turn our backs on the notion of perpetual contentment can only be a theoretical move; it has never really existed in practice. It is not in the nature of humankind to be always content, otherwise we would still be swinging in the trees. Some will argue that it would be better that way. The history of art and science demonstrates of what remarkable progress humankind is capable. However, the works or discoveries of very many of those who have played a key role in that progress were not born from contentment with their lot. What would have happened if pioneers like Galileo and Einstein had not been drawn back time and again into profound contemplation of a problem, if researchers like Madame Curie had not risked their lives in the pursuit of knowledge? Would the work of a writer like Heinrich von Kleist have come into being if he had been able to find salvation on earth? Would Vincent van Gogh have wielded his paintbrush with such passion if he had been at ease with himself and his art? Must one imagine Albert Camus, who reinterpreted the *Myth of Sisyphus* for our modern times, happy?

A large proportion of the wonderful things that the history of humankind has to offer did not arise out of contentment. The value of contentment as a life-goal is seriously overrated. *Dissatisfaction* is the spur to new deeds and discoveries — that is peculiar to humankind. "Only dissatisfaction makes us happy," wrote the musician and cabaret artist Georg Kreisler in his 2011 autobiography *Last Songs*. Perhaps only someone prone to doubt and despair is also capable of creating great and marvelous things. The contented person sits back and does nothing. We are fortunate inasmuch as dissatisfaction comes into being spontaneously when contentment outstays its welcome. That happens when an individual falls into a bad mood for no apparent reason; and it is the result of external influences that become challenges: Failures, setbacks, irritations, arguments and things that go wrong lead to periods of discontent that no one likes and that are inescapable nonetheless — to the horror of those who want nothing to do with them.

4

The Fullness of Life Consists in More than the Positive

No popular psychology handbook gets by without its mantra; at every turn one meets people who believe in it so absolutely that one is put in mind of a quasi-religion. *Positive thinking* has conquered Western culture in the last two or three decades. Not that it doesn't have positive aspects: It is encouraging, for example, when flooded by negative news to get a glimpse of land. One feels fresh vigor, new energies arise when things are not totally dominated by the negative. But why cling so fiercely to seeing the positive in all things? Why must each and every day be a positive day? Life is made up of quite different experiences, too, that serve to make the positive more precious. "Just Let Me Be the Sad One," sings German songwriter Michy Reincke on his 1993 album *Bad Happiness*:

Just let me be on my own,
Today all my joy is done,
Room for this feeling alone.

If a good mood is the only permissible mood, any moment spent out of sorts will become a major upset. The most unremarkable incident takes on a negative hue and one soon ends up tilting at windmills, for negativity spreads more quickly than any positive thinker can think positive thoughts. Trying to maintain a positive bent with all our strength soon saps us of our strength with the result that we try even more furiously to think positively. It's as if there is something inside us that needs to be kept in check. Perhaps that is a useful rule of thumb: The more we try to think positively, the more we get bogged down in the negative.

But can it really help to draw comfort from seeing things as they are *not*? Comfort of this sort cannot last. Positive thinking can inspire us to look at problems in a new light. However, it becomes part of the problem itself when it means seeing the positive to the exclusion of all else. Nothing is taken seriously in its own right any longer, everything becomes a question of perspective. Does it help someone who is seriously ill to believe at all costs that all will be well? I am haunted by the memory of a thirty-eight-year-old man who died of lung cancer. Right up until his very last breath he refused to think of his disease as fatal and firmly believed that he would beat it. He hadn't said his good-byes or even written a will — a fact that had unhappy consequences for his nearest and dearest.

That things and ways of being depend on how we perceive them was originally a discovery made by classical philosophers. It was Epictetus who said that it is in our power to construe the events of our lives, for an individual can interpret even unfortunate events such that they become livable. It is not what happens to us that is in itself depressing, but rather our attitude toward it. Not everything, however, can be turned to the good. Glasses are not always simply half full or half empty. They are sometimes completely empty. It is only by dint of recognizing that fact early enough that they can be filled up again in time. Crises are opportunities — we have all heard the slogan. But can they sometimes just be crises pure and simple? Debts can be put into a different context by a process of reframing, but can they be wiped out? It can happen that an individual is able to realize his ambitions purely by the power of his own positive thinking, but not every desire can be fulfilled without further ado; the ideal life he dreams of can never fully be made a reality.

"Keep looking forward" is the motto of those who think there is nothing to be learned from the past. Cultivating positive expectations and facing the future with optimism is not a bad resolution, but it can mean disregarding the negative and not being prepared for it in time. Positive thinking to the exclusion of all else undermines our sensibility for problems and for justified criticism; it is not a learning system and can turn out to be disastrous both at the individual and social levels. It is striking that no one

46

has pointed out the link to the totalitarian history of the twentieth century, which is so obvious: Infusing people with a positive outlook was also the agenda behind the National Socialist program of "strength through joy." No question that strength can be the result of joy, but a few questions would be appropriate with a view to limiting its misuse: Strength to do what? What joy? And what about those who cannot join in with the general rejoicing?

A more nuanced *art of living* demands that we sometimes see things in a positive light, but also look negative things squarely in the eye. We cannot believe blindly in the positive and become blind to the negative. Instead, we must ask critical questions and try to make things better. We must see not only the positive in the negative but the negative in the positive. Instead of hoping blithely that things will work out if only we think about them in a positive way for long enough, it is vital that we meet problems head on and start looking for practical solutions. That is the quickest way to get oneself out of a mess; otherwise it will take rather longer.

Isn't a person who thinks of all the things that can go wrong first in fact in danger of bringing them about in a kind of *self-fulfilling prophecy*? Those who believe that are the same people who believe that positive things will become real solely by dint of believing in them. One of the methods employed by classical philosophy rested not only, however, on positive interpretation, but also on considering all the unpleasant possibilities in advance, so that one cannot be suddenly caught out unawares. If the negative thing does then actually occur, the person is prepared and life goes on. If it doesn't come to pass it is all the more gratifying, and this pleasant situation, which would have gone unnoticed before, can now be consciously enjoyed. People who think negatively in this way, then, either discover that their fears are grounded or find that things turn out better than they had hoped. Stubbornly thinking only of the positive can mean that one is in for nasty surprises.

The catalogue of sins we can ascribe to positive thinking is a long one. While stalwart positive thinkers consider even harmless negative emotions to be highly infectious "emotional viruses," positive thinking is itself very infectious in a literal sense. Many people get infected with potentially fatal viruses simply because they believe nothing can possibly happen to them, so take no precautions and thereby also endanger others. A masterstroke of positive thinking can be seen in the poisoned financial institutions of the early years of the twenty-first century — both among those who invented them in the hope of profits, and those who got drawn into them along the way. A never-ending sequence of financial crises, economic crises, and crises of state were set in motion because too many people were fixed on the positive and stubbornly refused to listen to all the dire forecasts, of which there were plenty, and the warnings that grew ever louder. But reality cannot be spun at will.

The doom-mongers are not always right either, otherwise the world would have ended several times over. It is the one-dimensionality of positive or negative thinking that cannot do justice to the multidimensional world we live in. The *art of living* must encompass both sides of life, not only the positive, pleasant and enjoyable, but also the negative, unpleasant and painful we encounter and must deal with every day. Nobody goes looking for these things but they cannot be eliminated. It's a question of embracing a different kind of happiness; one that encompasses the full panoply of life – not only the happy accidents and a sense of wellbeing, but also the dark side of happiness, which must be taken into account at the most basic level.

This *happiness of plenitude* is dependent on a person stopping for a moment and thinking: What is life about? Isn't it the case that life rests on polarities; oscillates between opposites and contradictions like success and disaster, achievement and failure, joy and anger, courage and fear, pleasure and pain, health and illness, satisfaction and disappointment, good cheer and misery? Our modern concept of the world and man has long been based on perfectibility – the idea that one day everything will be strictly positive. And yet there are negative things that will not go away. Other cultures have a different view: "We don't have this idea of a perfect life that cannot be destroyed," said the Indian novelist Arundhati Roy in a 2011 interview.

This polarity also defines those human relationships in which people sooner or later come to feel unhappy. Mostly it is blamed on the other, who is no longer perfect in the way he was when we first met him. In that case leaving and finding a new partner is always an option. But what if unhappiness is unavoidable, even after several new partners, because it is simply part and parcel of the whole business at least once in a while, what then? Relationships aiming for the happiness of permanent wellbeing come to grief quite quickly. Truly *meaningful* relationships on the other hand, as when the partners view each other as a community of fate, will be able to weather even unhappy times. The key question is this: Can I be in accord with the polarity of life at its most basic level — even if not with each and every event? Each of us has to find his own answer. Only if we acquiesce in this fundamental given can unhappiness also be part of life and love. If we are lucky, it can be controlled, but that depends on its right to existence being acknowledged at the outset.

The happiness gained from life's fullness is a *breathing happiness*, because even happiness has to be able to breathe. No one can only ever inhale; one has to exhale before one can inhale again. In this way one can move between the poles of the negative and the positive, using the things that go well to draw new breath — especially in difficult times when life seems to be closing in — and being prepared when one is on top that there will be worse times to come. Only the entire gamut of experiences between the two poles makes for a truly fulfilled life. This is to all intents and purposes philosophical happiness (in its fullest sense) — one that does not

depend on favorable or unfavorable circumstances or the momentary fluctuations between
wellbeing and unease. This kind of happiness is,
as was already recognized by classical philosophy, an enduring happiness. Moreover, it can encompass being depressed, which is a widespread
form of unhappiness.

5
Being Depressed: Melancholia

Being depressed, in the dumps or weighed down by some kind of psychological burden has in the majority of cases nothing to do with the illness known as depression, and does not take on clinical characteristics. Everyday terminology is as inexact here as medical specificity, but in general being *depressed* is not the same as suffering from *depression*. Traditionally both black moods and being depressed have been called *melancholia*. Many of those diagnosed with depression are in fact melancholy. They have a tendency to feel blue; they don't suffer from the illness. Melancholy is a way of being, a mode of existence of the soul that belongs to the experience of being human at its very core, without being pathological in any way. Human life is marked not only by *joy* but by *sorrow*, not only laughter but tears too; everything to its own time. In the Old Testament Book of Ecclesiastes (7, 3) sorrow is even preferred to laughter, as this experience "makes the heart glad." Through sorrow we come to know ourselves from a new and mysterious side, and come to know others in a new way too. Fair-weather friends are suddenly busy elsewhere, while others who have been less assiduously jolly are the ones on whom you can count.

There are out-and-out times of melancholy. You are doing something wrong in life if, as a teenager, you are not assailed by melancholy when you look back at lost childhood or watch the autumn leaves fall and the trees grow bare. Whether the mood will pass or last a long time is not always clear at the start. In many cases it can be overcome, though there is no golden rule that it should be — self-help books aside. It can have many causes, those that stem from the moment, or deep-seated, long-lasting ones. People "fall into depression" when they lose something that has meaning for them — a relationship, a job. But also when they fail to obtain something they have set their heart on. But they even get depressed when their deepest desires are fulfilled and an unexpected void opens up inside them. Someone who has achieved his goal is not prepared for the fact that all his efforts and sacrifices now bring tears to his eyes, and all the tension simply evaporates.

It makes us depressed that the world seems to be peopled by idiots (ourselves, of course, excepted). We are cast down when we feel unjustly treated or experience disappointment, disdain, humiliation or violence. None of these have to be accepted, but equally none of them can be effectively eliminated forever. People become deeply unhappy when they do not feel liked or loved, when they have to give up their loved ones, or are deserted by them. But, above all, when they or those precious to them are confronted with illness or perhaps even death.

Key events in life can be marked by pain that cannot always be lessened or alleviated. And the *weltschmerz* occasioned by the world and by life as we know it is as inconsolable as it is inexplicable. Even without a cause that can be pinned down at any given moment, this feeling can be perfectly reasonable; all it takes for us to feel unhappy is the awareness that our life span is limited, that we will one day have to leave this life and our loved ones behind. Nothing lasts forever; everything is transient, and what has gone cannot be brought back. That everything must pass is an unalterable fact of life.

The quintessential *loneliness of existence* is in itself painful. Nothing can alter that. Perhaps this insight has been common throughout history, but it becomes stronger in times when the notion of self becomes stronger too. *I am* living this life, no one else. *I have* to endure the sight of the abyss opened up by unhappiness and misfortune. *I will* die alone; no one can do it for me. And these are *my thoughts* about what lies beyond, important only to me. Others may think differently, and there is nothing that unites us, if not love, friendship, or at least affection.

Wondering – for some that's already tantamount to being depressed. The melancholy reflect on everything, that's why there are so many philosophers and artists among them. That it is chiefly thinking, creative people who are the subjects of melancholy was already proposed by classical Aristotelians. In modern times psychological research has confirmed that people with depressive tendencies approach intellectual tasks more thoroughly and come to more intelligent conclusions. They scrutinize things for longer and more closely and are not distracted from their purpose by the need to see everything through rose-tinted glasses. They recognize the uncertainty of that which appears certain and understand the dubious nature of all things. They have no illusions about the doubtful nature of human action and how meaningless human existence can be. They are touched and moved by the possible tragedy of life. The risk they run is not that they might regard things too superficially, but rather that they might not be able to escape the depths, that they might see their own "identity" crumble and become alienated from themselves.

Melancholy, however, is not only character-ized by an overwhelming flood of thoughts, but also by extreme and uncontrollable emotions. Very few perceive in this turbulence a form of happiness, but it does in any case offer *meaning*. If life presents us with extreme states of feeling, we cannot only experience the positive ones: joy, love and ecstasy. Without experiencing the full reach of our emotional life, we cannot enjoy the fullness of life. Perhaps that is the root cause of dejection that appears groundless on the sur-face: "Actually everything is fine, I don't know what's the matter with me." A life that knows only harmony needs dissonance. Obstinate *joie de vivre* can be exhausting and needs the kind of respite offered by mourning. In order to tap the full potential of human existence and to live life to the full, we must savor melancholy down to the very last drop, even though that might at first seem counterintuitive.

Can people be deliberately melancholy? Yes, no question about it – inasmuch as they call painful memories to mind, whose pain never

truly goes away: the pain of separation from a
loved one, for instance. And there is always the
amorphous pain of *weltschmerz* that can be con-
jured to order – on account of the transience of
life and all things, perhaps even the world itself,
though it is difficult to pinpoint, even with the
aid of science. Melancholy can be summoned
voluntarily in order to balance out the positive,
restore the polarity of life and keep happiness
in check. It is given expression in the famous
song by Friedrich Hollaender, sung by Marlene
Dietrich in 1931:

> If I could wish something for me
> I'd wish to be just a bit happy
> For if I were too happy
> I'd be homesick for misery.

6
Depression: The Illness

Clinical depression is characterized by a feeling of oppression, quite different from the emotional and intellectual agitation of melancholy, and features atrophied feelings, general apathy and a genuine incapacity for reflection. A simple conversation quickly establishes the difference. The person concerned cannot escape the narrow compass of his own thoughts and is at the end of his tether, no longer able to manage the simplest tasks. He needs people around him who, with his consent, will take on responsibility for him; relatives and friends who will be there for him, behavioral therapists and analysts who will treat him, and doctors who will bring the very best of contemporary medicine to bear.

The fact that a diagnosis of *depression* is now ever more frequently made for what is in fact melancholy means that numbers have reached absurd proportions. This is helpful in improving public awareness of the illness, but not in determining the appropriate treatment for the individual. A person in the grip of melancholy does not really need medication as a first line treatment, but someone to talk to; a person who is clinically depressed needs a doctor and a proper course of treatment. Medication can influence the metabolization of the hormone serotonin; supplements can be used to make up for what the body lacks, especially vitamin D. In Northern climes, in particular, vitamin D deficiency plays a part in the not always entirely harmless SAD syndrome. There is also the issue of organic problems that can either be a cause of depression or result from it: for example, thyroid malfunction, which causes problems for the regulation of hormone release.

More difficult is the *grey area* between melancholy and depression, in medical terms: between mild and severe depressive episodes that can both, moreover, be marked by psychotic symptoms. Where exactly does the clinical illness begin? A *depressive reaction* can occur as a result of acute or chronic situations of stress, and might have its roots in past traumatic experiences that can develop into neuroses. An *endogenous depression*, on the other hand, can occur within a patient without any sign of an external trigger and can alter brain processes, possibly also on account of a pre-existing genetic predisposition. A *masked depression* can be disguised by pain and physical symptoms. A *manic-depressive illness* catapults sufferers more or less violently between phases of manic hyperactivity and depressive morbidity, "now shouting for joy, now plunged into deadly sorrow," to quote Goethe.

A diagnosis of depression often overlaps with that of *burnout*. Indeed, often the latter is actually preferable, as it sounds more positive: You have worked too hard, possibly even sacrificed your health for others – for your family, employer, society (that it might just be "your own fault" remains unspoken). This kind of exhaustion, too, ranges over a wide spectrum between the condition of melancholy, which is part and parcel of life, and clinical depression, which in the worst scenario can be life-threatening. Each kind has specific consequences: For *everyday exhaustion*, a bit of time out is all that's needed, some rest and recuperation, lessons in how to be kinder to oneself, to take care of oneself and treat oneself a little better. In cases of *total exhaustion* that becomes chronic, the treatment can be a good deal more protracted. In order to be able to take up their lives again sufferers need the continued support of others.

The causes of this modern epidemic of exhaustion are often identified as the complexity of today's personal relationships and the stress of our modern workplace environments. Didn't these also exist in times gone by? Look at Antonio, in Shakespeare's *Merchant of Venice*: "In sooth, I know not why I am so sad." Is he not suffering from chronic exhaustion? He doesn't know what has caused him to feel this way and has no name for it, so does not believe himself entitled to feeling as he does. For many people a term or label is the prerequisite that allows a reality to come into being; as soon as a label is there, they rush to locate their reality under its umbrella. Perhaps this is one of the functions of the term 'burnout': to give a purchase on reality as people experience it, and to allow them to respond to it. Defining it as an illness gives sufferers permission to be exhausted and to recuperate. However, the causes of exhaustion in modern times could also be different from those in the past, and effective therapies will have to address them.

An increasing number of people in modern society lack *meaning*, in all areas and at all levels: meaning in their work, meaning in their own lives, meaning in life itself. Meaning gives strength; meaninglessness saps it. If people can see the sense of something, they can bear a good deal and overcome a good deal more. Without it, they can do very little. Once people thought they could detect providence in fate, a higher order. They did not go chasing after meaning but drew it from the world around them, the familiar and reliable relationships with one another, but also with a higher instance beyond the human realm. As the modern age has seen many of the traditional founts of meaning run dry, there has been an ever more urgent call to find it again. Material comfort cannot deliver a satisfactory answer to the question of existence, unless it is clear what *ideal purpose* it serves such that meaning and energy can be gained from it. Any attempt to fill this vacuum with material things does little more than provoke anxiety, as these things could be lost at any moment. So where can people find meaning today?

They hope to find it in happiness. But happiness is no substitute for meaning, and especially not the transient happiness brought about by feeling good. In the final analysis, the urgency of the search for happiness is an index of the despair caused by the absence of meaning. When the stresses and strains of modern life, love and work deplete all our energies, the prospect of happiness is used to mobilize our last reserves. Do people have any sense of what awaits them? In order to avoid crisis at all costs they go in desperate pursuit of happiness, hence the constant refrain. But that creates a further kind of stress: the *stress of happiness*. People are ready to do anything for happiness, without realizing how it is precisely this that saps all their energies. This kind of happiness does not breathe, it does not encompass the richness of life; exhaustion is not kept at bay by this kind of happiness. Instead, it is promoted. The single-minded pursuit of the positive, of happiness in this sense, can drive people to burnout.

On the other hand, feeling unhappy could be the very thing that prompts reflection, a timely reminder of the need for meaning. Seen in this light, what does it tell us about our society that unhappiness itself is often viewed as a kind of illness? Who in truth is ill in this scenario? Why should someone go to any lengths to pick himself up out of the slough of despond without delay, even turning to fast-acting medication? Why should someone who is feeling bad do everything in his power in order to "feel better" as quickly as possible? Shouldn't he rather take a moment to consider, reorient himself, ask what is going wrong in his life, his surroundings, or in society at large, and how he can start to put things right once he is strong again? Both melancholy moods and clinical depression can be accompanied by suicidal thoughts. With the difference that those given to depressive moods tend simply to play with the idea, dwelling on it for a long time, and weighing up the arguments pro and contra. For those who are clinically depressed, it is far more likely that they are not playing and have little interest in the various arguments. Rather, they will simply find themselves at some point determined to die and to take the final step, whatever happens.

7

Living on the Edge of the Abyss

Someone who is entertaining thoughts of suicide can of course refuse to speak about it with anyone else; that is his prerogative. But the key is trying to reach out to the suicidal person nonetheless. The best starting point for the person who wants to help is fully accepting the situation. A person in the grip of depression sees problems at every turn; his whole attention is focused on the myriad difficulties to be surmounted, everything is alarming. The world and the people in it are full of contradictions, and they suffer from the knowledge that nothing can change that fact. It is not easy to live when all one sees is hopelessness. It is difficult to take a first step when the ground is collapsing all around and chasms open up at every turn. What remains is despair.

It is important to face the question of life and death head on, instead of meeting it with prohibitions and taboos, which are anyway ineffectual. The option of taking one's own life is open to us all in a fundamental way; and suicide is no longer categorized as murder, as in days of old. There is no shortage of premeditation, but there is no base motivation or malice involved. No one can be charged and convicted after the event. A human being is the only creature that can also refuse to live. There is no compulsion to live, no duty to stay alive. The choice of death by one's own hand is an option available to the *art of living*. Seneca's *Moral Epistles* dating from the first century AD already make that plain.

The basic questions can certainly also be addressed to those who want to carry on living: Do you really know what you are doing? Have you thought it through? Have you made a considered choice free of all constraints? Can life really be considered in and of itself as an "end in itself"? The existential choice to grant life this value is more credible if it is made against the backdrop of a possible rejection of life. It is only in the face of death that life acquires meaning and value, so that it is often the possibility of death that leads decisively to a choice for life. If one simply lives one's life without ever taking that fundamental step, one's life remains undefined, detached, superficial, and it never really becomes one's own. Is this kind of thinking dangerous? Doubtless the simple thought of suicide carries within it the danger that one might accede to it in a moment of doubt. But there is no life without risks of this kind.

The present context allows various fundamental questions about suicide to be aired properly. Is there such a thing as free choice in extremis? One's freedom to choose this step could be restricted. A *distortion of perspective* could be in operation, impinging on one's view of life, so that it sometimes seems black and completely meaningless, as when love fails, and sometimes seems bright and full of meaning, as in the first euphoria of love. What is life really like? That's not clear, but everything speaks for it being more than it seems to be at any given moment. There are always alternative perspec-

tives, and none of them can exhaust the multi-
tude of possibilities. It is of course possible to
base a decision with such far-reaching consequences on the feeling of the moment, but it is
not advisable.

How would it be if one ended up regretting
such a decision after the event? This might seem
unthinkable, but who can definitively exclude
the possibility of a hereafter that could be over-
shadowed by regret? In any case, the experience
of many who have at some point seen suicide as
their only remaining resort, but have made their
way through that crisis, tells us that in retrospect
they often consider their decision to be a moment of madness and are pleased that they did
not take the final step or were prevented from
doing so at the last moment.

Just as the experience of meaning is subject
to shifting perspectives, so too is the experience
of meaninglessness. Nothing in the world or life
has any meaning any longer? But none of us has
the complete overview of life or the world that
would allow us to say that with any final cer-

tainty. Basing the ultimate choice on a temporary mood has the hallmark of arbitrariness, and no degree of hopelessness, temporary or long-lasting, can disguise that. Suicide only appears less arbitrary when it comes as a response to the inescapable, in truth only when someone is facing an incurable illness or unbearable horror. And even then it should not be a spontaneous decision, but the result of mature reflection.

Suicide can be something undertaken *actively* even when it involves *passive euthanasia* as offered by the various organizations that make the necessary means available. But it can also be a *passive act*, as for example in the case of the Norwegian adventurer Thor Heyerdahl. In 2002, at the age of 87, he stopped taking in food, liquids or medication after being diagnosed with a brain tumor. In this way, he died a short time later at home in Italy.

Suicide is also *passive* when *voluntary euthanasia* is involved. But this choice, taken by an individual who is not capable of engaging in the necessary actions and depends on active assistance, brings with it very particular problems. Inevitably, this course of action draws others into a position of responsibility and for that reason requires legal regulation that addresses proper care and regard. For who is in a position to decide on a case-by-case basis whether the desire to die belongs to the invalid himself or to his relatives, who may have an eye on acceding to their inheritance and saving the costs of care? Active euthanasia is also the business of the mafia, which for good reasons neglects to question its candidates thoroughly on their motivations. For that reason legislation such as has been practiced in the Netherlands for many years offers a way forward: The desire to die must be voluntary, "well-considered," and persist over time, in order to ensure that it is not the result of a temporary emotional aberration. Doctors must independently confirm that the person seeking death is incurably ill and is no longer in a position to carry out the deed himself. Only then can the voluntary euthanasia take place and only with the help of a physician.

Reasonable criteria for this choice are, how-ever, dependent in the first place on two very specific considerations. *Consideration for one's self* leads to the question: Is it fair to do violence to the self and, in particular, to those aspects within it that are of a different opinion? And *consideration for others* demands that one ponder the question: Has enough thought been given to the consequences of this action for other people who are important to the individual concerned? Could they be adversely affected – in material or spiritual terms – through the death of the individual? Unless of course the object is to bequeath difficulties to others, to mark them for years to come, and to force them into endlessly interpreting and reinterpreting the death. For above all, this kind of death provokes an unassuagable disquiet in the living: Was it my fault? What did I do wrong? Did I miss something? What could I have done?

These could be taken as arguments in favor of trying to find a way through the situation in question. "Don't give up," goes a line in the 2003 song "New Morning," by the German pop group Blumfeld, in which many will find just the right words and the right tone for their situation. As an alternative, however, there is the prospect of a life that is *happy in a different way* — a life lived with unhappiness, a life that does not close itself to the despair that is a part of our everyday lives, but prevents those extremes of despair that in the long run act to undermine our very hold on life.

8
A Guide to Living with Unhappiness

What remains when everything seems pointless? Throwing in the towel and falling into despair – or reconciling oneself with this aspect of life and recognizing the potential for reclaiming meaning, despite all meaninglessness. All facets of human existence can become instruments in the search for meaning. Moments of happiness can be part and parcel of this, but meaning itself is something larger.

To find meaning in life we need to start with sensuousness, which we experience through our five senses of sight, hearing, smell, taste and touch, along with a sixth which is our sense of movement and a seventh inner sense – what we might call *gut instinct*. What we owe to these seven senses is a world that only 'makes sense' for this minute, this hour or this day. We are overwhelmed by the *sight* of something beautiful or beautifully sad, perhaps embodied in land-

scapes, whether real or imagined, or the land-
scape of a body, or most especially a face. A
wonderful *fragrance* can beguile our noses but
also make us sad, something which can be all the
more the case with a foul smell too. A tasty *meal*
always brings a little bit of meaning in the midst
of all unhappiness. And we glean real peace from
the experience of *touch*, which is nevertheless
something far too seldom used or afforded.

It does someone with a melancholy bent a
world of good to listen to *music* or indeed to play
it, for in music we find melancholy completely
comprehended. Its vibrations allow body, mind
and soul to come together in a single sound
space to celebrate the melancholy feelings and
thoughts. A good proportion of music across the
ages, from the classical poems of Sappho to
modern pop, consists of fragments of an artfully
composed misery. The Baroque *joie de vivre* of
Händel's *Music for the Royal Fireworks* is scarcely
conceivable without the subdued melancholy of
the Larghetto in his opera *Xerxes*. The music of
the Romantic era in fact favors the dark sides of

existence over lighter ones, which later ages saw as the dominant attribute of the "romantic." Johannes Brahms' song "In the Quiet Night" has the voices sing of the "bitter sorrow and grief" into which the "heart has melted."

One also begins to feel one's own energies return when one starts to *move* or take part in sports. Regular walks often bring relief from a brown study, as they allow one to dwell on dismal thoughts while at the same time taking in a whole world of sensory impressions. The rhythmic movement of *dance* also offers respite for the melancholy soul, and it might even welcome the company of another soul, too. There is that churning in the stomach that comes with an *erotic encounter*. The sensual charms of such an experience offer a counterpoint to melancholy and bring the polarities of life into harmony by redressing the negative experiences with positive ones. That erotic sensibilities are at their strongest precisely when the gloom is at its deepest is a fact certainly not lost on classical Aristotelians, for instance, who already pointed out, in the famous *Problema XXX.1*, that melancholy souls are often "lascivious." When life is hanging by a thread, the erotic impulse can sometimes be the strongest argument not to let it break. A moment of unity, whether dreamed of or real, can heal the suffering caused by separation, for a short time at least, notwithstanding the acute *tristesse* that may come in its wake.

Beyond bodily experience, one can be moved inwardly by the *nourishment* for one's *soul* provided by all kinds of relationship, not just in the moment but over long periods of time and perhaps even a lifetime. The soul can be understood as the place where the energies reside that make us who we are. They can be felt in the ups and downs of our emotional life, and they come to the fore in relationships. But there are always contradictory emotions in one and the same individual, so it is vital to be friends with *one's self* in order to counteract the inner divisions that can undermine our relationships with others. One of the most important anchors in one's life and unhappiness is one's *work*, which seems meaningful when it creates connections and is something one enjoys, even if it is not necessarily the same as what we do to earn our living. Then there are the *habits* we are fond of, which provide a context where unhappiness can be lived through safely.

A good deal depends on contexts in which contradictory feelings have their place. Someone with a melancholy disposition needs companions with whom he can share the whole range of his emotions. Then he can at least feel that even in moments of most profound isolation someone is there for him. *Lovers* whose relationship is solid despite the bad patches or arguments do not dwell on the question of meaning any longer; they already have an answer. *Friends* who feel close to one another find meaning in their relationship, which makes their lives better and adversity easier to bear. A sense of lasting meaning that provides a bulwark against unhappiness can be found in being part of the growing life of *children* in all their naturalness. Every kind of *socializing* can create

83

meaning out of the connections with others that are being ritually tended. And all kinds of *collaboration* appear more meaningful than a senseless laboring alongside one another.

Many people find in the sense of *Heimat* or *home(land)* a place of meaning and familiarity when they are unhappy. For others it is being somewhere unknown, where no one knows them so that they don't have to keep up any kind of appearance. And if a relationship or connection fails to ignite with another human being, perhaps an *animal* will provide the answer; showing it kindness and care so that life gains meaning again even when one is unhappy. Nourishment for the soul can be found in the experience of *nature*, where human beings can gain strength from recognizing the inter-connectedness of everything. Maintaining a *garden* can be helpful, or plants on a balcony, or even a window ledge, where something is growing. The cycle of growth and decay found in nature represents a form of time where a melancholy disposition can feel much more at home than in the accelerating linear time without return of our modern culture.

Happiness is knowing people with whom one can be totally open in times of unhappiness. A conversation with someone close also has the effect of creating *spiritual meaning*. Talking can help; silence rarely does unless it is the kind of silence between people who understand one another without words. It doesn't have to be an intellectual exchange; even a chat will do. Every conversation, however insignificant in itself, ties the threads that bind us together. It embodies meaning simply by dint of taking place, especially with those precious to us, but also with acquaintances, strangers and those who interact with us in a professional capacity. It is the attention given to us by others that does us so much good.

Of particular significance in the intellectual realm are *narrative links*. Everything that can be narrated makes sense. It is easier to stich the fragments of our lives and the various parts of our being back together again if we can tell

someone about ourselves. The most disparate
events and pieces of information come together
to create networks that only have to be halfway
plausible to appear meaningful to us. That is why
we are so fond of telling stories and of listening
to them. It keeps us from experiencing the abyss
of meaninglessness.

Meaning in an intellectual sense can also be
strengthened by an interest in alternative view-
points and possibilities of *interpretation*. On the
other hand, the fixation on incontrovertible
truths, often blind alleys, can be dangerous. A
good deal depends on the capacity to draw on
the accrued interpretative potential of a lifetime
in difficult situations so that one doesn't get
locked into supposedly irrefutable facts but can
always see things in another way, take a different
route and find a way out of the bottlenecks of
life and thought. Art and literature, education
and development offer inexhaustible material
for open-ended explanations and interpretations
that leave the way clear for further unseen and
unknown connections. The myriad available in-

terpretations even suggest that in life in fact everything is full of coherence and meaning.

What something is good for – what its aim is and what purpose it serves – is equally a matter of interpretation. Throughout history, humankind has drawn meaning from this kind of thinking. Perhaps it will be possible in due course to set oneself a goal despite the relativity inherent in all such goals. It could be a near or a distant goal. It could be a case of working towards the fulfillment of a small wish, or pursuing a great dream, and learning that the intensity of finally realizing that goal is in direct proportion to the length and difficulty of the journey. It is also possible to consciously do without goals or objectives, to take life as it comes and follow where it leads.

Engaging with life intellectually can also lead one to conclude that one of the contexts that ensure meaning is what might be termed *polarity*. Health without illness, joy without pain, life without death are unimaginable. Even the apparently contradictory aspects of life are often linked at a higher level, for example, the certainty of belief and the knowledge that all is open to question. Similarly, the fact that it is never just a question of what we consciously do or leave undone and bear responsibility for, but also those things that come about without volition and that no one is responsible for. Finally, that a nexus of inexplicable and indissoluble connections exists with which humankind must make its peace.

Melancholy as a Transcendental Ability

Does meaning continue to exist beyond the end of life? Those with a tendency to melancholy are at odds on this question, as, in many cases, the individual with himself. For some, the idea of meaning beyond the grave is unimaginable; and they respond by pinning their hopes on the meaning to be found in the realm of the senses. That is enough for them. For others, the question of transcendental meaning is beyond doubt; it is only life that has forfeited meaning. They embrace the wisdom of the chorus in Sophocles' *Oedipus at Colonus*: Never to have been born is best, but, once you've entered this world, the second best is to return as quickly as possible to the place you came from.

Even those melancholy souls who throw themselves into the sensual pleasures of the world still find that the limited world outside them remains fundamentally foreign. They feel that they carry another world within, whether dreamed or real, which is ancient, interior and infinite. This world full of energies and intensities gives rise to their very soul. And they believe that this energy, like all other known forms of energy, cannot be destroyed and is therefore immortal. It is within this soul, this profound inner self that, unlike the surface self, has no name, that they feel the essence of being human. The soul is the subtle, or completely immaterial, stuff that in the midst of this finite and mortal life provides a bridge to the realms of the infinite and immortal.

Of course for the most part we feel such infinite energies only in the painful recognition of their absence in our mortal lives. This brings suffering. The melancholy soul has no access to the inexhaustible energies vouchsafed by a life in the infinity of being; he can only sense them through the thin skin of his bodily finitude. And this is what makes melancholy a transcendental ability. Both in words and feelings it is a form of *crossing over*, transcendent in the literal sense of the Latin *transcendere*. The threshold it crosses is the very boundary of finitude; beyond it something other, something indeterminate opens up. For such people, a life of true intensity, *being* itself, is not to be found in this life, in *existence*, however attractive the here and now might be. The melancholy spirit means forever mourning the metaphysical gap between this world and the other, never finding a lasting home here, and being plagued by nostalgia for another realm to which one feels oneself called back. Melancholy is sorrow about the alienation of humankind from its immemorial origins; sorrow about the impossibility of finding anything but a fleeting union with others, which can still the longing for a moment in offering a pale imitation of that original intensity.

In this and other ways as well, those who tend towards melancholy also tend towards religion, even if they do not think of themselves as religious in any conventional way. Many prefer to call it *spirituality*; but even then it is above all a matter of remaining open to the Other, open to the unknown fate or mysterious sense that seems to reside there. In this case, it is not called God, but spirit (*spiritus* in Latin), though like God it is there to contain the unhappiness and misfortune that become intolerable if they do not find their place in the overarching whole where all is connected.

In the absence of *certainty*, access to this realm of meaning beyond finite life can be a matter of *conjecture*, which leaves the door open for all those who do not want to associate transcendence with belief of any kind. In this way, they need not reject the possibility of another dimension where the answers to the eternal questions about the origins and destiny of humankind and the world, the real meaning of it all, fate, determinism and existence, might be suspected to reside, though in truth they might have no place in that realm at all.

Such a breaking of boundaries can be played out at least as a *possibility*, a thought experiment, quite independently of physical reality. And this alone has the power to allow the subject to leave the narrow confines of his selfhood and this world behind him. Being able to imagine this possibility is a device learned from the *art of living*, in which the melancholy too are well-versed. The plenitude of life between real finitude and possible infinity brings comfort in the face of the poverty of the present, where the richness of life and the possibility of existential fulfillment are curtailed by the reality of the moment.

Being able to fill the subjectively experienced emptiness of existence with a projected meaning is a kind of *mysticism* that requires no final certainty but allows for a possible truth. One error we have encountered in the modern age is that of identifying the general idea of an undetermined, transcendent dimension with a particular version of that possibility and then rejecting it. As a result, the powers that can grow and develop out of the relationship to such a dimension have become painfully lacking. Was it *transcendental ignorance* that triggered the growing pressure to realize all our dreams in this one short life — there being no beyond to reckon with? Was it this that caused such intolerable suffering, as the realization dawned that all attempts to make these dreams come true in our finite lives were inevitably doomed to failure? Was it this that drove increasing numbers of people into the arms of melancholy?

But melancholy is not only the result of our inability to fulfill our dreams of unending intensity; it can also be a release from the very hope of fulfillment in this finite life of ours. Knowing that these things simply cannot be done frees us from our miserable efforts to cram everything into this, presumably *only*, life of ours. The coming time of melancholy might therefore also herald an age of new freedom.

10
The Dawning of the Age of Melancholy

Times of euphoria are followed by times quite different in nature; our euphoria about happiness is no exception. That could be one of the reasons why more and more people are in the grip of a melancholy that is totally new to them. The more the meaning of life is sought in a perpetual state of joy, the greater the disappointment when it fails. Even someone who sets out to radiate constant contentment will have enough of it after a while. Every fire burns itself out in the end, and all that remains is to poke about in the ashes for new material to burn.

The dream that has haunted the imagination since the beginnings of the modern age – the dream of the greatest happiness for the greatest number of people – was euphoric. The old idea of eternal salvation was transformed seamlessly into the modern idea of happiness. Even the poet Heinrich Heine wanted "to found heaven here on earth" and "to be happy on earth." But this world stubbornly refuses to become a paradise. The extent of the hopes placed in such happiness at the individual and social levels correlates with the letdown experienced when all efforts come to naught. The hubris of believing one can use science and technology to create lasting happiness naturally provokes the thought that all human striving is basically pointless. The historical experiences associated with the project of socialism, which once harbored so many hopes, could certainly be repeated in capitalism, which is founded on a very similar dream.

Those looking back on the first decades of the twenty-first century will be amazed: How could people in the throes of such monstrous national debt and absurd financial debacles be so obsessed with their own personal happiness? Did they have nothing else to worry about? But they turned to happiness precisely because they had other worries. They insisted on thinking positively because they hoped that way at least they themselves would find a way out. Very few indeed applied their positive thinking to the spread of globalization – as an opportunity to establish more just conditions in the developing world market, for example. An entire age must have been extremely desperate to think positively, indeed in direct proportion to its deteriorating conditions. However, confronted by the hopelessness of the enterprise of creating a wholly positive world, it was above all the rhetoric used to conjure it that grew in intensity.

The withdrawal into a niche society, into private happiness, is understandable as a vital reflex to escape the growing demands from the outside world and to keep the encroaching pressures of unhappiness at arm's length: at last a little bit of happiness. As the demands grow ever more extreme, this kind of refusal becomes a seductive alternative. By attending to their inner world, people form a fold in the fabric of society, as it were, where they can live turned in on themselves in the true sense of the word, in the midst of a time that is accelerating uncontrollably. In a culture that has experienced a huge burst of evolutionary acceleration across time and space, the happiness people are looking for is nothing but the memory of a different world without time, where life was sheltered, at least in their imagination.

But melancholy is not simply the result of waking from the dream of happiness. The new mood of sorrow stems from a sense of impending catastrophe and that is why the new age of melancholy will be like no other before. More and more people are recognizing the *ecological* disaster that threatens us all. They see it hurtling towards them like the planet *Melancholia* in Lars von Triers' 2011 film of the same name, set on a collision course with earth. A nightmare made real and threatening to overtake humankind. For too long people have blindly believed that the costs of modern life and economic development were worth paying. But it is becoming clear that younger generations will be left having to deal with the ever-increasing problems inherited from previous generations with no trace left of all those great hopes for human happiness. Autumn is drawing in for the planet as a whole, the time of great sorrow. Even in spring in the midst of all the green and blossoming, melancholy is budding too. How long will things continue to be like this? How long will human beings be around to witness this?

The reasons for the dawning of the age of melancholy stem from the fear that humankind might disappear; not as a result of an atomic flash or a cosmic thunderclap, but by dint of a disaster creeping up on us – and which, with the best will in the world, it may no longer be possible to halt. Floods will lay waste to humankind; people will drown in the torrents of filth, brought down by the force of the elements they themselves have unleashed. After all, is there any persuasive argument that humankind should actually exist?

And yet it is enough to make one weep when one thinks that the decision about our future will be made only by a tiny proportion of humankind, and what is more, in a kind of daze.

For this situation where people can see perfectly well what should be done but simply fail to do it can hardly be called consciousness. It is a sorry situation that the rest of humanity will bear the consequences too, that all the children and children's children to come will think back on their forbears with horror; forbears who were not prepared to keep the existence of future generations in mind even though they were constantly mouthing the word "future" at every turn. The problems are manifest. But the individual feels he can achieve nothing alone, is reluctant to be the first one to act, and shifts responsibility onto the shoulders of others. Out of this feeling of impotence in the face of the powerful, but even more in the face of our own inaction, comes melancholy and depression. In the final analysis, the crippling sense of our own powerlessness leads to the sense that things have already gone too far to be put right.

The important thing is not whether these dismal predictions are right. No one can say for certain whether things will really pan out like this. It might be that such a vision results from a limited view that takes a few problems for the whole picture. Though it was, of course, also a limited view that brought about the extent of the ecological crisis in the first place. For a long time, worrying signs were greeted with pacifying answers: Wait and see, collect more data and so on. But at the point at which it is crystal clear which way things are heading, it is too late to formulate a response. This hopeless situation, this potential snuffing out of human existence, is one reason for the *metaphysical melancholy* of the coming time. Even if we are only dealing with one small world in the infinite reaches of the cosmos, the meaningless existence of one creature in this tiny corner of the universe, isn't it nevertheless a pity that this should come to pass?

The significance of the melancholy of the coming time might, as in previous times, reside in the possibility it brings of gaining reflexive distance and exposing the dangerous way people take things for granted without really noticing they are doing so. The realization that we find ourselves in a dangerous situation may become the trigger that makes people take stock and renew the search for meaning. It conveys the experience of groundlessness that is nevertheless fundamental, in that it makes us aware of the meaninglessness inherent in the human state and that the ground can disappear from under our feet at any moment.

A possible answer to this dilemma is the renewed attention to meaning in the form of goals and objectives. For many centuries, the task of defining such goals belonged to *heteronomous* authorities within church, state and society. In the modern age, that task has increasingly devolved to financial institutions, whose goals, unfortunately, are limited to the pursuit of economic growth and the conquering of new markets. For *autonomous* modern individuals it must become part of their conscious living, their *art of living*, to reflect on which goals and aims can open meaningful perspectives that would allow them to follow a given path of their own free will, even if, all things being equal, they would have wanted to go a different way. The kind of perspective available to an individual, but which simultaneously points far beyond him, could, for example, be the opportunity to work towards an ecologically sustainable and socially just society and world society, linked with the constant readiness to scrutinize one's own actions and omissions and to ask which contribute positively and which do not.

Are we to fear revolt and revolution on this path, or indeed to hope for them? Revolution is not the forte of melancholy souls. Their strength is their *sensitivity*, their fine antennae for meaning and its absence; this is their gift to society at large. Such sensitivity is the only human capacity that promises any hope of salvation. For this reason alone, the flip side of happiness is not without purpose: The unhappy notice danger, wrong turnings, injustice and inequity far more readily than the happy. Unlike optimists, for whom the sight of someone brought low with the weight of care is simply an obstacle to their positive world-view, melancholy people are apt to offer compassion — providing encouragement in being unhappy.

If grounds for unhappiness are compounded by grounds for *indignation*, even those of a melancholy bent can rouse themselves to action. They are not doing it for themselves, mind you, in order for example to create better conditions where they can leave their melancholy behind. It is too much part of who they are. But the prospect that human life might be improved for others gives them no rest. In contrast to the optimists, they are in no doubt that the fate of humanity is that of Sisyphus, doomed to keep on hauling the stone to the top, only to see it roll down again. They are ready and willing to take on the efforts involved in making things better, even as elsewhere things are patently getting worse. This means there is always something to do. Can this make people happy? Possibly. And maybe precisely when unhappiness can be accepted as a real possibility of being human.

About the Author

Bestselling author Wilhelm Schmid is the most significant and popular contemporary German moral philosopher. In his many books on topics such as 'happiness', 'love', the 'meaning of life', and 'balanced living' – to name only a few – he has been endeavoring to create a *philosophy of the art of living* for our time. He has been awarded the German Prize for Outstanding Services in Conveying Philosophy to the Public (2012) and the Swiss Prize for his Philosophical Contribution to the Art of Living (2013). Translated into numerous languages, Wilhelm Schmid's books have sold over 800,000 copies worldwide. He lives in Berlin, Germany, and travels around the world giving lectures and workshops on the *philosophy of the art of living*.

About the Translator

Award-winning author and translator Karen Leeder is Professor of Modern German Literature at the University of Oxford and a Fellow New College, Oxford.

Also Available from UWSP

- *November Rose: A Speech on Death* by Kathrin Stengel
  (2008 Independent Publisher Book Award)

- *November-Rose: Eine Rede über den Tod*
  by Kathrin Stengel

- *Philosophical Fragments of a Contemporary Life*
  by Julien David

- *17 Vorurteile, die wir Deutschen gegen Amerika und die
  Amerikaner haben und die so nicht ganz stimmen können*
  by Misha Waiman

- *The DNA of Prejudice: On the One and the Many*
  by Michael Eskin (2010 Next Generation Indie Book
  Award for Social Change)

- *Descartes' Devil: Three Meditations* by Durs Grünbein

- *Fatal Numbers: Why Count on Chance*
  by Hans Magnus Enzensberger

- *The Vocation of Poetry* by Durs Grünbein
  (2011 Independent Publisher Book Award)

- *The Waiting Game: An Essay on the Gift of Time*
  by Andrea Köhler

- *Mortal Diamond: Poems* by Durs Grünbein

- *Yoga for the Mind: A New Ethic for Thinking and Being
  & Meridians of Thought* by Michael Eskin & Kathrin
  Stengel

- *Health is in Your Hands: Jin Shin Jyutsu – Practicing the
  Art of Self-Healing (With 51 Flash Cards for the Hands-
  on Practice of Jin Shin Jyutsu)* by Waltraud Riegger-Krause

- *A Moment More Sublime: A Novel* by Stephen Grant

- *Potentially Harmless: A Philosopher's Manhattan*
  by Kathrin Stengel

- *Become a Message: Poems* by Lajos Walder

Made in the USA
Monee, IL
11 May 2024

58328704R00062